SCHOLASTIC

GRADES
K-2

FIRST COMPREHENSION:
FICTION

25 Easy-to-Read Story Pages
With Just-Right Questions

IMMACULA A. RHODES

W9-BAA-447

New York • Toronto • London • Auckland • Sydney
Mexico City • New Delhi • Hong Kong • Buenos Aires

Cover design: Tannaz Fassihi; photo: © asiseeit/Getty Images; illustration: Jannie Ho
Interior design: Michelle H. Kim; Interior illustration: Mattia Cerato

Scholastic Inc., 557 Broadway, New York, NY 10012
ISBN: 978-1-338-31433-5
Copyright © 2019 by Scholastic Inc.
All rights reserved.
Printed in the U.S.A.
First printing, January 2019.

1 2 3 4 5 6 7 8 9 10   131   25 24 23 22 21 20 19

Contents

Traditional Tales

First Comprehension: Fiction © Scholastic Inc.

Introduction

Welcome to *First Comprehension: Fiction!* The 25 realistic fiction, fantasy, and traditional tales in this collection were developed to boost reading comprehension skills. The easy-to-read tales include repetition, decodable and high-frequency words, predictable patterns, and picture clues to aid in fluency so children can focus on the meaning of what they read. Reproducible comprehension activities let children check their understanding by answering age-perfect questions, responding to true/false items, and drawing informative pictures.

The texts in each category increase in difficulty, giving you the flexibility to meet the needs of children at different ability levels. They are correlated with guided reading levels A–E. (See page 7 for the specific level of each story.) Each text is paired with a comprehension activity page that children complete to demonstrate their understanding of what they have read. The items include important skills, such as identifying main ideas and details, sequencing, making predictions and inferences, understanding cause and effect, and more.

You can use the texts and comprehension activities for whole-class, small group, or one-on-one comprehension instruction. The sample lesson plan (see page 8) provides a framework for introducing and modeling reading in a meaningful context, as well as for after-reading discussion and completing the comprehension activities. The texts also work well as learning-center or take-home activities. Best of all, the activities support children in meeting the reading standards for Literary and Foundational Skills for grades K–2. (See Connecting to the Standards, page 9.)

How to Use

The texts and companion activity pages in this book are ideal for use as part of your instruction in comprehension. Research shows that comprehension instruction can help all readers including emergent and struggling readers, improve comprehension by understanding, remembering, and communicating with others about what they read. Improved comprehension also creates greater enjoyment in reading, so children will want to read more!

Preparing to use these texts for comprehension instruction is as easy as 1, 2, 3! Simply make copies of a selected text and comprehension activity for each child, distribute the pages, then follow the sample lesson on page 8 to guide your instruction. You'll see that the sample lesson is very similar to an interactive read-aloud in which fluent, expressive reading is modeled while teaching the reading process in a meaningful context. The steps guide you to encourage higher levels of thinking and questioning that will help children develop understanding of the text, build vocabulary and background knowledge, and make connections to prior knowledge, self, and the world.

Teaching Tips

- Prior to the lesson, preview the text to become familiar with it.

- Identify any vocabulary that might need to be introduced.

- Enlarge the text page and display it so that everyone has a clear view of the text and illustrations.

- As you ask purposeful questions, remember that "why" and "how" questions prompt deeper thinking about the meaning of the text.

- Encourage children to ask questions and share their understanding of the text.

- Invite children to retell the story.

- Work with the whole class, small groups, or individuals to complete the comprehension page. Before children begin to fill in the page, read aloud each item and have children follow along. They can then go back and work on their own.

- As needed, model how to complete the short answer and true/false sections of the comprehension page.

- Allow children to dictate their responses to items on the comprehension page.

Learning Centers

Place copies of the desired text and comprehension pages in a folder. During their turn at the center, have children take a copy of each page and independently work through the text and comprehension activity. To make the activity self-checking, enlarge the answer key for the corresponding comprehension page and staple that page to the inside of the folder. When children complete the activity, they can check their responses by referring to the answer key.

Ways to Use the Texts

The texts and companion comprehension activities are ideal for the following:

- Whole-class instruction
- Small-group instruction
- One-on-one lesson
- Learning center activity
- Individual seatwork
- Take-home practice

Correlated by a team of guided reading specialists.

Sample Lesson

Follow the steps below to provide comprehension instruction for the text of your choice.

1. Display a copy of the text page, making sure everyone can see it. Use sticky notes to cover each of the four panels on the page.

2. Point out and read the title. Ask: "What do you think this text will be about?" Encourage children to share their predictions.

3. Take a quick picture walk through the panels, but do not read the text. Reveal one panel at a time, starting with the first panel and ending with the last. This allows children to see the pictures in sequence so they can start constructing meaning.

4. Invite children to share what they know about the text topic, based on their predictions and the picture walk. This helps them relate to the text and sets the stage for making additional predictions and connections as the lesson continues. Also, introduce any unfamiliar or difficult vocabulary words from the text.

5. Read the text aloud. Use lots of expression, animation, and enthusiasm to engage children. Pause to ask purposeful questions and check children's understanding of the text and pictures. Model a think-aloud process to encourage understanding and thinking beyond the text and to explore vocabulary. For example, "I wonder why the character did that"; "I think this word means _____ because _____"; and "That reminds me of _____." Invite children to share their own comments, questions, and observations during the read-aloud.

6. After reading, talk about the details and main points of the text. Encourage children to share their understanding of the text.

7. Review the comprehension page with children before having them complete it. Encourage children to write their short answer responses in complete sentences and to refer to the text to check their work. Afterward, invite them to share and discuss their responses.

First Comprehension: Fiction © Scholastic Inc.

Connecting to the Standards

The lessons in this book support the College and Career Readiness Anchor Standards for Reading for students in grades K–12. These broad standards, which serve as the basis of many state standards, were developed to establish rigorous educational expectations with the goal of providing students nationwide with a quality education that prepares them for college and careers. The chart below details how the lessons align with specific reading standards for literary and informational texts for students in grades K through 2.

Foundational Skills

Print Concepts

- Demonstrate understanding of the organization and basic features of print.

- Follow words from left to right, top to bottom, and page by page.

- Recognize that spoken words are represented in written language by specific sequences of letters.

- Understand that words are separated by spaces in print.

- Recognize and name all upper- and lowercase letters of the alphabet.

- Recognize the distinguishing features of a sentence (e.g., first word, capitalization, ending punctuation).

Phonics and Word Recognition

- Know and apply grade-level phonics and word analysis skills in decoding words.

- Demonstrate basic knowledge of one-to-one letter-sound correspondences.

- Associate the long and short sounds with the common spellings for the five major vowels.

- Distinguish between similarly spelled words by identifying the sounds of the letters that differ.

- Decode regularly spelled one-syllable words.

- Know final -e and common vowel team conventions for representing long vowel sounds.

- Use knowledge that every syllable must have a vowel sound to determine the number of syllables in a printed word.

- Recognize and read grade-appropriate irregularly spelled words.

Fluency

- Read emergent-reader texts with purpose and understanding.

- Read grade-level text orally with accuracy, appropriate rate, and expression on successive readings.

- Use context to confirm or self-correct word recognition and understanding, rereading as necessary.

Literary Skills

Key Ideas and Details

- Ask and answer questions about key details in a text.

- Retell familiar stories, including key details.

- Identify characters, settings, and major events in a story.

- Describe characters, settings, and major events in a story, using key details.

Craft and Structure

- Ask and answer questions about unknown words in a text.

- Name the author and illustrator of a story and define the role of each in telling the story.

- Identify who is telling the story at various points in a text.

Integration of Knowledge and Ideas

- Describe the relationship between illustrations and the story in which they appear.

- Compare and contrast the adventures and experiences of characters in familiar stories.

Range of Reading and Level of Text Complexity

- Actively engage in group reading activities with purpose and understanding.

Source: © Copyright 2010 National Governors Association Center for Best Practices and Council of Chief State School Officers. All rights reserved.

First Comprehension: Fiction © Scholastic Inc.

Kip Rides

1
Kip rides on a train.

2
Kip rides on a plane.

3
Kip rides on a boat.

4
Kip rides on a horse.
Yeehaw!

Name: _____

WRITE!

1. Who is the story about?

_____
_____
_____
_____
_____

2. What does Kip ride first?

_____
_____
_____
_____
_____

SHADE!

1. Kip rides on a bus.

TRUE   FALSE

2. Kip rides on a boat.

TRUE   FALSE

DRAW!

Which ride has legs?

First Comprehension: Fiction © Scholastic Inc.

My Silly Cat

1

My silly cat plays with my cars.

2

My silly cat plays with my blocks.

3

My silly cat plays with my crayons.

4

My silly cat plays with my toes. Hee-hee!

First Comprehension: Fiction © Scholastic Inc.

Name: _____

WRITE!

1. What animal is this story about?

_____

_____

_____

_____

_____

2. Why is the cat silly?

_____

_____

_____

_____

_____

SHADE!

1. The cat plays with dolls.

TRUE   FALSE

2. The cat plays with crayons.

TRUE   FALSE

DRAW!

What four things did the cat play with?

At the Beach

1 Pam saw happy kids at the beach.

2 Pam saw happy birds at the beach.

3 Pam saw happy fish at the beach.

4 Pam saw crabby crabs at the beach. Oh, my!

Name: _____

WRITE!

1. Where is Pam?

_____

- -

_____

_____

- -

_____

2. Which animals were happy at the beach?

_____

- -

_____

_____

- -

_____

SHADE!

1. Pam saw a fish jump out of the water.

(TRUE)   (FALSE)

2. Pam saw a frog jump out of the water.

(TRUE)   (FALSE)

DRAW!

Which animals were crabby at the beach?

Nell Gets Ice Cream

1 Nell gets one scoop of ice cream.
One!

2 Nell gets two scoops of ice cream.
One, two!

3 Nell gets three scoops of ice cream.
One, two, three!

4 Oops! Nell gets two scoops of ice cream.
Her dog gets one scoop of ice cream.

Name: _____

WRITE!

1. Who is the story about?

_____

_____

_____

_____

2. Why did the dog get one scoop of ice cream?

_____

_____

_____

_____

SHADE!

1. At the end of the story, Nell got one scoop of ice cream.

TRUE   FALSE

2. At the end of the story, Nell got two scoops of ice cream.

TRUE   FALSE

DRAW!

How many scoops did Nell have before one fell off?

Time for Bed!

1

Time for bed!
Bob puts on his pajamas.

2

Time for bed!
Bob brushes his teeth.

3

Time for bed!
Bob reads a book.

4

Time for bed!
Zzzzzzzzzz!

18

WRITE!

1. Why did Bob put on his pajamas?

_____
- -
_____
_____
- -
_____

2. What happened to Bob at the end of the story?

_____
- -
_____
_____
- -
_____

SHADE!

1. Bob brushed his teeth.

TRUE   FALSE

2. Bob brushed his hair.

TRUE   FALSE

DRAW!

What does Bob do in bed?

The Squirrel

1 Peg saw a squirrel by the tree.

2 The squirrel went up the tree. It ate a nut.

3 The squirrel ran over to a bush. It ate a berry.

4 The squirrel ran over to Peg. It ate her apple!

First Comprehension: Fiction © Scholastic Inc.

Name: _____

WRITE!

1. What did Peg see by the tree?

_____

_____

_____

_____

2. What did the squirrel do in the tree?

_____

_____

_____

_____

SHADE!

1. The squirrel ran over to a boy.

TRUE   FALSE

2. The squirrel ran over to a bush.

TRUE   FALSE

DRAW!

What three things did the squirrel eat?

Our Class Pets

1

Our class has a pet
rabbit.
It likes to eat carrots.
Crunch, crunch, crunch!

2

Our class has a pet
turtle.
It likes to eats bugs.
Crunch, crunch, crunch!

3

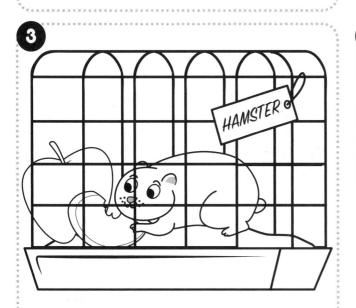

Our class has a pet
hamster.
It likes to eats apples.
Crunch, crunch, crunch!

4

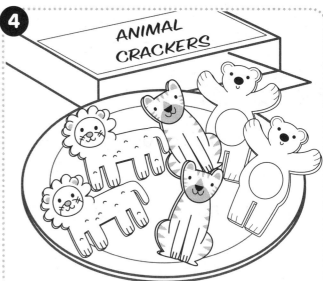

Our class has lions,
tigers, and bears, too.
We like to eat those.
Crunch, crunch, crunch!

Name: _____

WRITE!

1. What pets does the class have?

_____
_____
_____
_____
_____

2. What does the hamster like to eat?

_____
_____
_____
_____

SHADE!

1. The turtle eats animal crackers.

TRUE   FALSE

2. The class eats animal crackers.

TRUE   FALSE

DRAW!

What do the turtle and
the rabbit eat?

Fun at the Park

1

The sun came out.
Kim and Sam went
to the park.
"Hooray!" said Kim
and Sam.

2

A cloud came out.
Kim and Sam played
on the slide.
"We love to slide!"
said Kim.

3

More clouds came out.
Kim and Sam played
on the swings.
"We love to swing!"
said Sam.

4

The rain came down.
Kim and Sam played
in the puddles.
"We love to splash!"
said Kim and Sam.

First Comprehension: Fiction © Scholastic Inc.

Name: _____

WRITE!

1. Where did Kim and Sam go?

_____

_____

_____

_____

2. How did the puddles get there?

_____

_____

_____

_____

SHADE!

1. Kim and Sam played on a rock.

TRUE   FALSE

2. Kim and Sam played on a slide.

TRUE   FALSE

DRAW!

What did Kim and Sam do in the rain?

A Bike for Pat

1 Pat got a new helmet.

2 Pat got a new horn.

3 Pat got a new basket.

4 Pat got a new bike. Go, Pat!

Name: _____

WRITE!

1. What did Pat get first?

_____

_____

_____

_____

2. What did Pat get last?

_____

_____

_____

_____

SHADE!

1. Pat rode a new bike.

TRUE   FALSE

2. Pat rode a new swing.

TRUE   FALSE

DRAW!

What two things did Pat put on her bike?

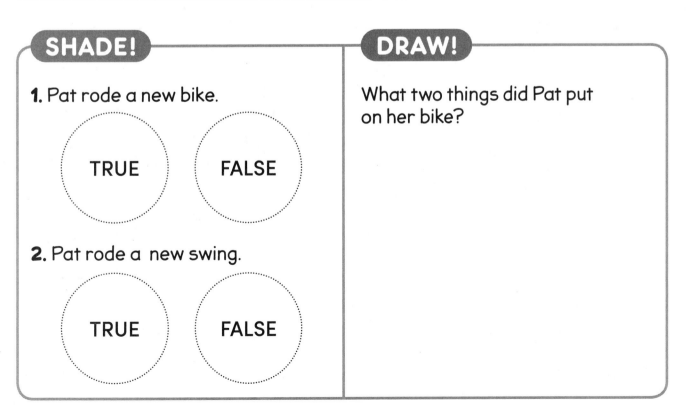

Fish School

1 Min loves her school. She can swim!

2 Min loves her school. She can jump!

3 Min loves her school. She can flip!

4 Min loves her school. She can read!

First Comprehension: Fiction © Scholastic Inc.

Name: _____

WRITE!

1. How does Min feel about her school? How do you know?

_____
_____
_____
_____
_____

2. How is fish school like your school?

_____
_____
_____
_____
_____

SHADE!

1. Min loves to sing at her school.

(TRUE)   (FALSE)

2. Min loves to read at her school.

(TRUE)   (FALSE)

DRAW!

What does Min take to school with her?

Big, Scary Mouse

1
Look at that shadow!
Mouse looks big.

2
Look at that shadow!
Mouse looks scary.

3
Look at that shadow!
Mouse looks big and
scary.

4
Mouse is not big.
Mouse is not scary.

Name: _____

WRITE!

1. Who is the story about?

_____

_____
_____

_____

2. How does Mouse's shadow look?

_____

_____
_____

_____

SHADE!

1. Mouse is a big animal.

TRUE   FALSE

2. Mouse is a small animal.

TRUE   FALSE

DRAW!

What animal did mouse see?

The Flying Dragon

1

The dragon flew over
a big mountain.
Fly, fly!

2

The dragon flew over
a big lake.
Fly, fly!

3

The dragon flew into
a big castle.
Fly, fly!

4

Thank you!

The dragon lit a big fire.
The queen was happy!
Happy, happy!

WRITE!

1. What did the dragon do first?

_____

_____

_____

_____

2. Why was the queen happy?

_____

_____

_____

_____

SHADE!

1. The dragon flew over a big lake.

TRUE   FALSE

2. The dragon flew over a big garden.

TRUE   FALSE

DRAW!

Who did the dragon light the fire for?

Ted From Zed

1 This is Ted from Zed.
Ted took a trip.

2 He went by the stars.
Hello, stars!

3 He went by the moon.
Hello, moon!

4 He went down to Earth.
Hello, friends!

WRITE!

1. Where is Ted from?

_____

- -

_____

- -

_____

2. What happens at the end of the story?

_____

- -

_____

- -

_____

SHADE!

1. Ted took a trip in a plane.

TRUE   FALSE

2. Ted took a trip in a space ship.

TRUE   FALSE

DRAW!

What two things did Ted fly by on his trip?

Monster Soup

1 This monster is Meg.
She is making soup.

2 Meg puts in worms.
She puts in rocks, too.

3 Meg puts in wheels.
She puts in socks, too.

4 Meg eats up the soup.
"Yum, yum!" she says.

WRITE!

1. What is the monster making?

_____

- -

_____

- -

_____

2. How do you know the monster likes her soup?

_____

- -

_____

- -

_____

- -

_____

SHADE!

1. The monster's name is Meg.

TRUE   FALSE

2. The monster's name is Kim.

TRUE   FALSE

DRAW!

What 4 things does the monster put in her soup?

Time to Fly

1

Mother came to
Will, Jill, and Bill.
"It is time to fly,"
she said.

2

"Look! I can fly!"
said happy Will.
"Not me," said sad Bill.

3

"Look! I can fly!"
said happy Jill.
"Not me," said sad Bill.

4

Bill got a leaf.
Then he jumped.
"Look! Now I can fly!"
said happy Bill.

WRITE!

1. What did Mother tell the baby birds?

_____

_____

_____

_____

2. Who was the first baby bird to fly?

_____

_____

_____

_____

SHADE!

1. Bill was the last baby bird to fly.

TRUE   FALSE

2. Jill was the last baby bird to fly.

TRUE   FALSE

DRAW!

What did Bill use to fly?

The Loose Tooth

1

Meet Rex.
Rex had a loose tooth.
He wiggled his tooth
all day at school.
Wiggle, wiggle.

2

Rex wiggled his tooth
all day at the park.
Wiggle, wiggle.

3

Rex wiggled his tooth
all day at home.
Wiggle, wiggle.

4

FOR THE
TOOTH FAIRY

The tooth came out!
Rex wiggled his tail
all night in bed.
Wiggle, wiggle.

WRITE!

1. Why did Rex wiggle his tooth?

_____
- -
_____
_____
- -
_____

2. Why did Rex put his tooth in a box with a note?

_____
- -
_____
_____
- -
_____

SHADE!

1. Rex is a kitten.

TRUE   FALSE

2. Rex is a puppy.

TRUE   FALSE

DRAW!

What did Rex lose?

My Robot

1

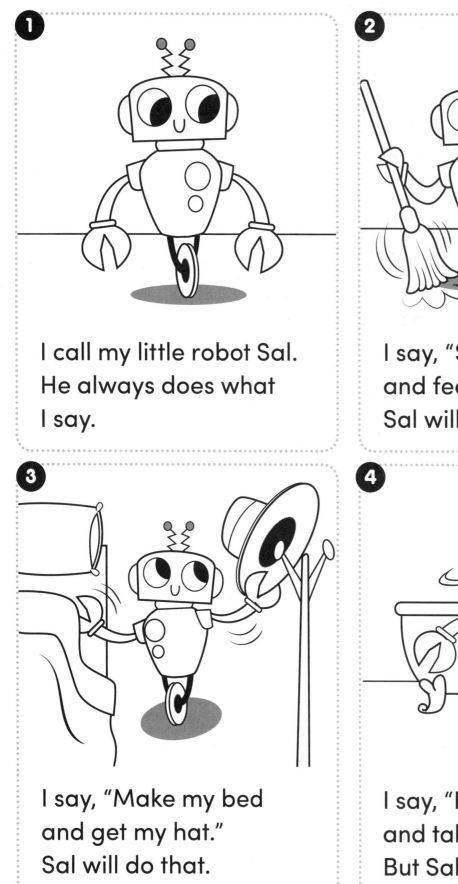

I call my little robot Sal.
He always does what
I say.

2

I say, "Sweep the floor
and feed the cat."
Sal will do that.

3

I say, "Make my bed
and get my hat."
Sal will do that.

4

I say, "Fill the tub
and take a bath."
But Sal will NOT do that!

Name: _____

WRITE!

1. What is the name of the robot?

_____

_____

_____

_____

2. What does the robot do to the bed?

_____

_____

_____

_____

SHADE!

1. Sal feeds a dog.

(TRUE)   (FALSE)

2. Sal feeds a cat.

(TRUE)   (FALSE)

DRAW!

What will Sal NOT do?

The Gingerbread Man

1. The man chased the Gingerbread Man.

2. The pig chased the Gingerbread Man.

3. The cow chased the Gingerbread Man.

4. CRUNCH!

   The fox ate the Gingerbread Man.

Name: _____

WRITE!

1. Who chased the Gingerbread Man first?

_____

- -

_____

_____

- -

_____

2. What two animals chased the Gingerbread Man?

_____

- -

_____

_____

- -

_____

SHADE!

1. The Gingerbread Man was a cookie.

TRUE   FALSE

2. The Gingerbread Man was a cake.

TRUE   FALSE

DRAW!

Who ate the Gingerbread Man?

Goldilocks

1

Goldilocks ate
from three bowls.
One, two, three!

2

Goldilocks sat
in three chairs.
One, two, three!

3

Goldilocks slept
on three beds.
One, two, three!

4

Goldilocks ran
from three bears!
One, two, three!

Name: _____

WRITE!

1. What did Goldilocks sit in?

_____
_____
_____
_____
_____

2. How did Goldilocks sleep in?

_____
_____
_____
_____
_____

SHADE!

1. The house belonged to three dogs.

TRUE   FALSE

2. The house belonged to three bears.

TRUE   FALSE

DRAW!

What did Goldilocks do at the end of the story?

The Three Little Pigs

One little pig made
a straw house.
The wolf blew.
The house fell down.

One little pig made
a stick house.
The wolf blew.
The house fell down.

One little pig made
a brick house.
The wolf blew.
The house did NOT fall
down.

The wolf blew and
blew and blew.
Then HE fell down!

First Comprehension: Fiction © Scholastic Inc.

Name: _____

WRITE!

1. What two houses did the wolf blow down?

_____

_____

_____

_____

2. What house did the wolf NOT blow down? Why?

_____

_____

_____

_____

SHADE!

1. One little pig made a stick house.

TRUE   FALSE

2. One little pig make a stone house.

TRUE   FALSE

DRAW!

What happens to the wolf at the end of the story?

The Frog Prince

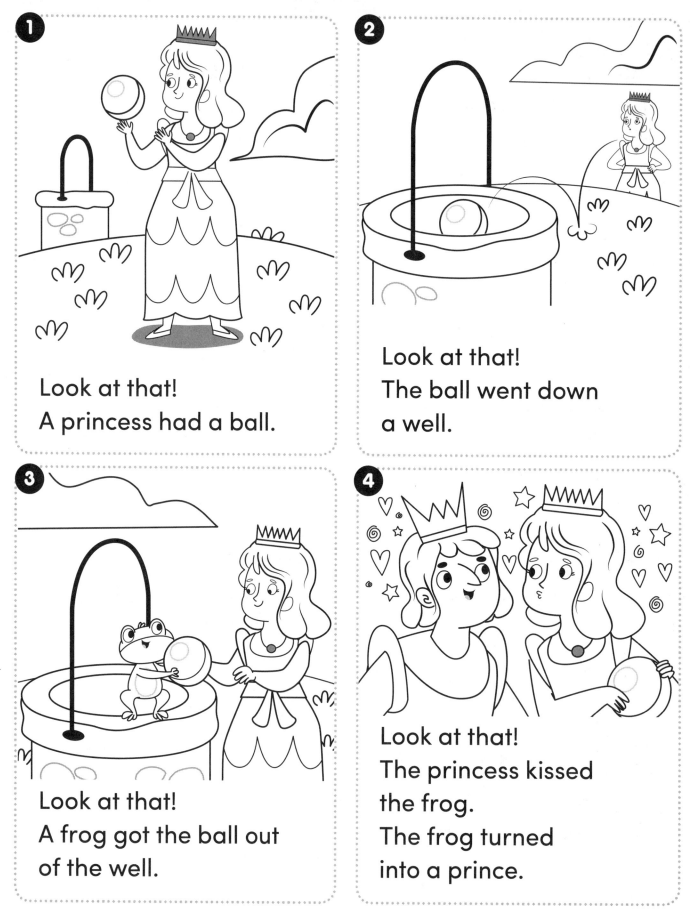

1 Look at that!
A princess had a ball.

2 Look at that!
The ball went down
a well.

3 Look at that!
A frog got the ball out
of the well.

4 Look at that!
The princess kissed
the frog.
The frog turned
into a prince.

Name: _____

WRITE!

1. What did the princess have?

_____

- -

_____

_____

- -

_____

2. Where did the ball go?

- -

_____

_____

- -

_____

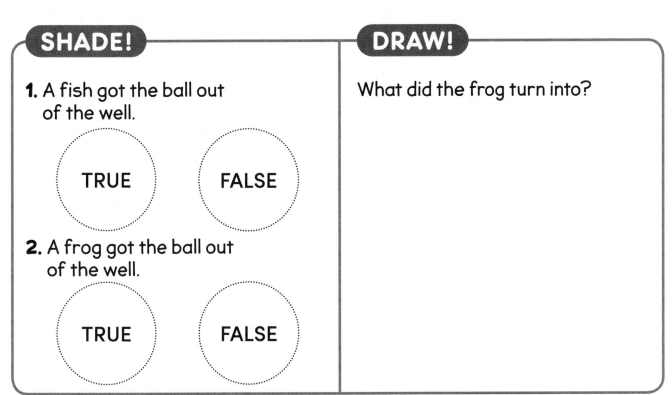

SHADE!

1. A fish got the ball out of the well.

TRUE   FALSE

2. A frog got the ball out of the well.

TRUE   FALSE

DRAW!

What did the frog turn into?

The Troll and the Goats

1

Three goats tried
to cross a bridge.
Clomp, clomp, clomp!

2

A mean troll jumped out.
Stop, stop, stop!

3

The big goat pushed
the troll off the bridge.
Splash, splash, splash!

4

The three goats
crossed the bridge.
Clomp, clomp, clomp!

Name: _____

WRITE!

1. Who tried to cross the bridge?

_____

- -

_____

_____

- -

_____

2. What stopped the goats?

_____

- -

_____

_____

- -

_____

SHADE!

1. The big goat pushed the troll off the bridge.

TRUE   FALSE

2. The little goat pushed the troll off the bridge.

TRUE   FALSE

DRAW!

What did the goats do last?

First Comprehension: Fiction © Scholastic Inc.

Paul and Babe

1

Paul Bunyan had
a big blue ox.
He named her Babe.

2

Babe helped Paul
chop down big trees.
Chop, chop!

3

Babe helped Paul
dig a big hole.
Dig, dig!

4

Babe helped Paul
make a big lake.
Time to swim.
Splash, splash!

Name: _____

WRITE!

1. What did Paul name his big ox?

_____
_____
_____
_____

2. What did Paul and Babe dig?

_____
_____
_____
_____

SHADE!

1. Paul and Babe chopped down flowers.

TRUE   FALSE

2. Paul and Babe chopped down trees.

TRUE   FALSE

DRAW!

What did Paul and Babe do in the lake?

Rapunzel

1

Rapunzel was locked
in a tower.
She had very long hair.

2

A prince called
up to the tower.
"Rapunzel, let down
your hair!"

3

Rapunzel let down
her hair.
The prince climbed up
her hair.

4

The prince helped
Rapunzel climb out
of the tower.
The two lived happily
ever after.

Name: _____

WRITE!

1. What was Rapunzel's problem?

_____

- -

_____

_____

- -

_____

2. Who came to help Rapunzel?

_____

- -

_____

_____

- -

_____

SHADE!

1. Rapunzel lived in a cave.

(TRUE)   (FALSE)

2. Rapuzel lived in a tower.

(TRUE)   (FALSE)

DRAW!

How did the prince get up the tower?

Jack and the Bean Plant

1

This is Jack.
He planted a magic bean.

2

A bean plant grew.
Jack went up the plant.

3

Jack found a hen
at the top.
The hen laid golden
eggs!

4

Jack went down the
plant with the hen.
Then Jack had lots of
golden eggs.
Hooray!

Name: _____

WRITE!

1. What did Jack plant?

_____

- -

_____

_____

- -

_____

2. What did Jack take with him down the bean plant?

_____

- -

_____

_____

- -

_____

SHADE!

1. Jack went up and down a slide.

TRUE   FALSE

2. Jack went up and down a bean plant.

TRUE   FALSE

DRAW!

What did Jack have lots of at the end of the story?

Answer Key

Name: Jason R. — Kip Rides

WRITE!

1. Who is the story about?

The story is about Kip.

2. What does Kip ride first?

The first thing Kip rides is a train.

SHADE!

1. Kip rides on a bus.
TRUE **FALSE**

2. Kip rides on a boat.
TRUE **FALSE**

DRAW!

Which ride has legs?

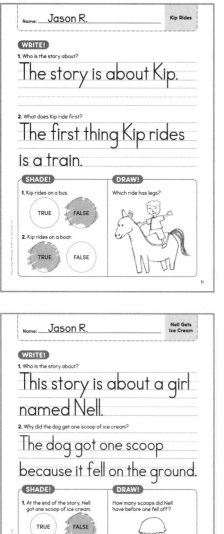

11

Name: Jason R. — My Silly Cat

WRITE!

1. What animal is this story about?

The story is about a silly cat.

2. Why is the cat silly?

The cat is silly because it plays with toes!

SHADE!

1. The cat plays with dolls.
TRUE **FALSE**

2. The cat plays with crayons.
TRUE **FALSE**

DRAW!

What four things did the cat play with?

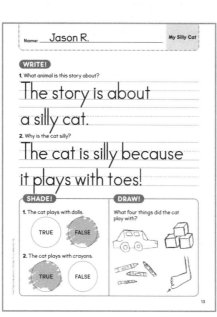

13

Name: Jason R. — At the Beach

WRITE!

1. Where is Pam?

Pam is at the beach.

2. Which animals were happy at the beach?

The birds and fish were happy at the beach.

SHADE!

1. Pam saw a fish jump out of the water.
TRUE FALSE

2. Pam saw a frog jump out of the water.
TRUE **FALSE**

DRAW!

Which animals were crabby at the beach?

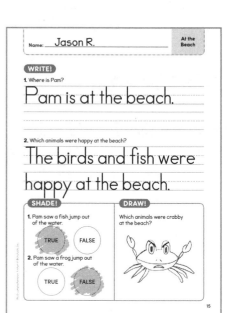

15

Name: Jason R. — Nell Gets Ice Cream

WRITE!

1. Who is the story about?

This story is about a girl named Nell.

2. Why did the dog get one scoop of ice cream?

The dog got one scoop because it fell on the ground.

SHADE!

1. At the end of the story, Nell got one scoop of ice cream.
TRUE **FALSE**

2. At the end of the story, Nell got two scoops of ice cream.
TRUE FALSE

DRAW!

How many scoops did Nell have before one fell off?

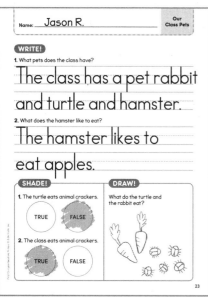

17

Name: Jason R. — Time for Bed!

WRITE!

1. Why did Bob put on his pajamas?

Bob put on his pajamas because it is time for bed.

2. What happened to Bob at the end of the story?

Bob fell asleep in his bed.

SHADE!

1. Bob brushed his teeth.
TRUE FALSE

2. Bob brushed his hair.
TRUE **FALSE**

DRAW!

What does Bob do in bed?

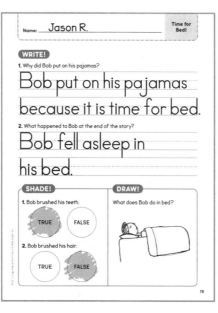

19

Name: Jason R. — The Squirrel

WRITE!

1. What did Peg see by the tree?

Peg saw a squirrel by the tree.

2. What did the squirrel do in the tree?

The squirrel ate a nut in the tree.

SHADE!

1. The squirrel ran over to a boy.
TRUE **FALSE**

2. The squirrel ran over to a bush.
TRUE FALSE

DRAW!

What three things did the squirrel eat?

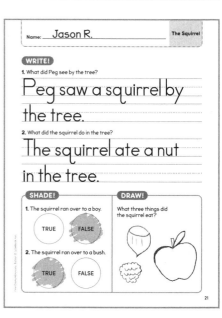

21

Name: Jason R. — Our Class Pets

WRITE!

1. What pets does the class have?

The class has a pet rabbit and turtle and hamster.

2. What does the hamster like to eat?

The hamster likes to eat apples.

SHADE!

1. The turtle eats animal crackers.
TRUE **FALSE**

2. The class eats animal crackers.
TRUE FALSE

DRAW!

What do the turtle and the rabbit eat?

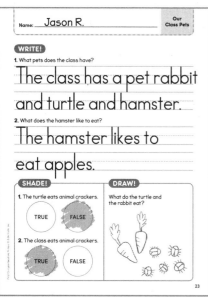

23

Name: Jason R. — Fun at the Park

WRITE!

1. Where did Kim and Sam go?

Kim and Sam went to the park.

2. How did the puddles get there?

The puddles got there because it rained.

SHADE!

1. Kim and Sam played on a rock.
TRUE **FALSE**

2. Kim and Sam played on a slide.
TRUE FALSE

DRAW!

What did Kim and Sam do in the rain?

25

Name: Jason R. — A Bike for Pat

WRITE!

1. What did Pat get first?

The first thing Pat got was a new helmet.

2. What did Pat get last?

The last thing Pat got was a new bike.

SHADE!

1. Pat rode a new bike.
TRUE FALSE

2. Pat rode a new swing.
TRUE **FALSE**

DRAW!

What two things did Pat put on her bike?

27

60

First Comprehension: Fiction © Scholastic Inc.

Answer Key

Name: Jason R. | Fish School |

WRITE!

1. How does Min feel about her school? How do you know?

Min loves her school. I know because she is smiling.

2. How is fish school like your school?

Fish school is like my school because we read books.

SHADE!

1. Min loves to sing at her school.
   TRUE **FALSE**

2. Min loves to read at her school.
   TRUE FALSE

DRAW!

What does Min take to school with her?

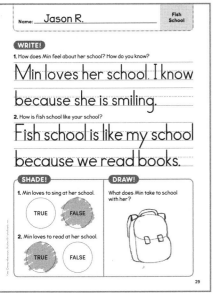

29

Name: Jason R. | Big, Scary Mouse |

WRITE!

1. Who is the story about?

The story is about Mouse.

2. How does Mouse's shadow look?

Mouse's shadow looks big and scary.

SHADE!

1. Mouse is a big animal.
   TRUE **FALSE**

2. Mouse is a small animal.
   TRUE FALSE

DRAW!

What animal did mouse see?

31

Name: Jason R. | The Flying Dragon |

WRITE!

1. What did the dragon do first?

The first thing the dragon did was fly over a big mountain.

2. Why was the queen happy?

The queen was happy because the dragon lit a big fire.

SHADE!

1. The dragon flew over a big lake.
   TRUE FALSE

2. The dragon flew over a big garden.
   TRUE **FALSE**

DRAW!

Who did the dragon light the fire for?

33

Name: Jason R. | Ted From Zed |

WRITE!

1. Where is Ted from?

Ted is from Zed.

2. What happens at the end of the story?

Ted went down to Earth and saw two friends.

SHADE!

1. Ted took a trip in a plane.
   TRUE **FALSE**

2. Ted took a trip in a space ship.
   TRUE FALSE

DRAW!

What two things did Ted fly by on his trip?

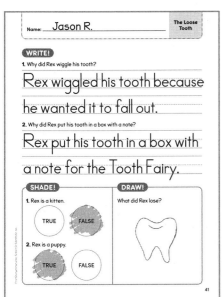

35

Name: Jason R. | Monster Soup |

WRITE!

1. What is the monster making?

The monster is making soup.

2. How do you know the monster likes her soup?

I know the monster likes the soup because she says, "Yum, yum!"

SHADE!

1. The monster's name is Meg.
   TRUE FALSE

2. The monster's name is Kim.
   TRUE **FALSE**

DRAW!

What 4 things does the monster put in her soup?

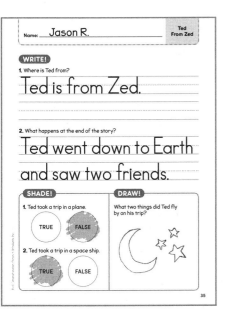

37

Name: Jason R. | Time to Fly |

WRITE!

1. What did Mother tell the baby birds?

The Mother told the baby birds that it was time to fly.

2. Who was the first baby bird to fly?

Will was the first baby bird to fly.

SHADE!

1. Bill was the last baby bird to fly.
   TRUE FALSE

2. Jill was the last baby bird to fly.
   TRUE **FALSE**

DRAW!

What did Bill use to fly?

39

Name: Jason R. | The Loose Tooth |

WRITE!

1. Why did Rex wiggle his tooth?

Rex wiggled his tooth because he wanted it to fall out.

2. Why did Rex put his tooth in a box with a note?

Rex put his tooth in a box with a note for the Tooth Fairy.

SHADE!

1. Rex is a kitten.
   TRUE **FALSE**

2. Rex is a puppy.
   TRUE FALSE

DRAW!

What did Rex lose?

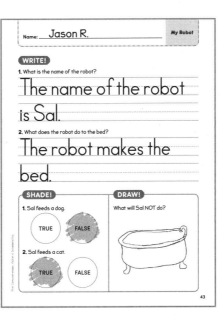

41

Name: Jason R. | My Robot |

WRITE!

1. What is the name of the robot?

The name of the robot is Sal.

2. What does the robot do to the bed?

The robot makes the bed.

SHADE!

1. Sal feeds a dog.
   TRUE **FALSE**

2. Sal feeds a cat.
   TRUE **FALSE**

DRAW!

What will Sal NOT do?

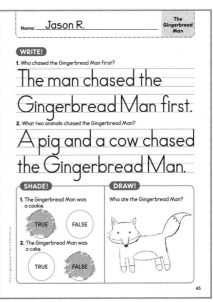

43

Name: Jason R. | The Gingerbread Man |

WRITE!

1. Who chased the Gingerbread Man first?

The man chased the Gingerbread Man first.

2. What two animals chased the Gingerbread Man?

A pig and a cow chased the Gingerbread Man.

SHADE!

1. The Gingerbread Man was a cookie.
   TRUE FALSE

2. The Gingerbread Man was a cake.
   TRUE **FALSE**

DRAW!

Who ate the Gingerbread Man?

45

Answer Key

Goldilocks — Jason R.

WRITE!

1. What did Goldilocks sit in?

Goldilocks sat in three chairs.

2. How did Goldilocks sleep in?

Goldilocks slept in three beds.

SHADE!

1. The house belonged to three dogs.
   TRUE / **FALSE**

2. The house belonged to three bears.
   TRUE / FALSE

DRAW!
What did Goldilocks do at the end of the story?

47

The Three Little Pigs — Jason R.

WRITE!

1. What two houses did the wolf blow down?

A straw and stick house got blown down by the wolf.

2. What house did the wolf NOT blow down? Why?

The wolf did not blow down the brick house because it was strong.

SHADE!

1. One little pig made a stick house.
   TRUE / FALSE

2. One little pig make a stone house.
   TRUE / **FALSE**

DRAW!
What happens to the wolf at the end of the story?

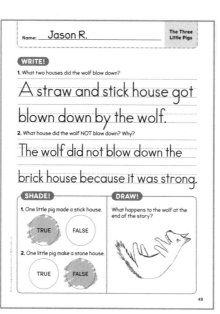

49

The Frog Prince — Jason R.

WRITE!

1. What did the princess have?

The princess had a ball.

2. Where did the ball go?

The ball went down a well.

SHADE!

1. A fish got the ball out of the well.
   TRUE / **FALSE**

2. A frog got the ball out of the well.
   TRUE / FALSE

DRAW!
What did the frog turn into?

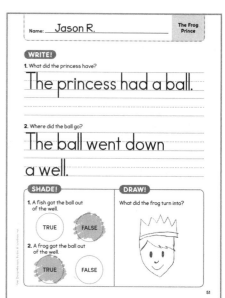

51

The Troll and the Goats — Jason R.

WRITE!

1. Who tried to cross the bridge?

Three goats tried to cross the bridge.

2. What stopped the goats?

A mean troll stopped the goats.

SHADE!

1. The big goat pushed the troll off the bridge.
   TRUE / FALSE

2. The little goat pushed the troll off the bridge.
   TRUE / **FALSE**

DRAW!
What did the goats do last?

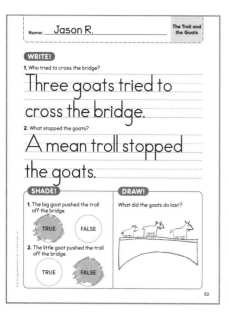

53

Paul and Babe — Jason R.

WRITE!

1. What did Paul name his big ox?

Paul named his big ox Babe.

2. What did Paul and Babe dig?

Paul and Babe dug a big lake.

SHADE!

1. Paul and Babe chopped down flowers.
   TRUE / **FALSE**

2. Paul and Babe chopped down trees.
   TRUE / FALSE

DRAW!
What did Paul and Babe do in the lake?

55

Rapunzel — Jason R.

WRITE!

1. What was Rapunzel's problem?

Rapunzel's problem was that she was locked in a tower.

2. Who came to help Rapunzel?

A prince came to help Rapunzel.

SHADE!

1. Rapunzel lived in a cave.
   TRUE / **FALSE**

2. Rapunzel lived in a tower.
   TRUE / FALSE

DRAW!
How did the prince get up the tower?

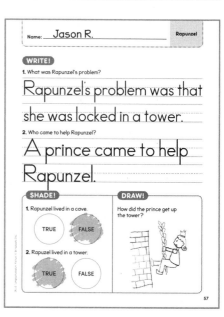

57

Jack and the Bean Plant — Jason R.

WRITE!

1. What did Jack plant?

Jack planted a magic bean.

2. What did Jack take with him down the bean plant?

Jack took a hen down the bean plant.

SHADE!

1. Jack went up and down a slide.
   TRUE / **FALSE**

2. Jack went up and down a bean plant.
   TRUE / FALSE

DRAW!
What did Jack have lots of at the end of the story?

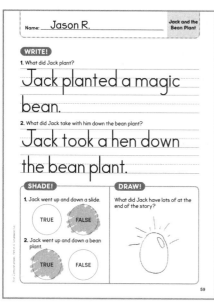

59

Notes

Notes